The Gift of Holy Communion

For Parents of Children Celebrating First Eucharist

Mary Kathleen Glavich, SND

ACTA
ASSISTING CHRISTIANS TO ACT
PUBLICATIONS

The Gift of Holy Communion
For Parents of Children Celebrating First Eucharist
by Mary Kathleen Glavich, SND

Edited by John Van Bemmel
Cover design by Tom A. Wright
Typesetting by Desktop Edit Shop, Inc.

Published by: ACTA Publications
                 5559 W. Howard St.
                 Skokie, IL 60077
                 www.actapublications.com
                 800-397-2282

Library of Congress Catalog Number: 2001094297

ISBN 10: 0-87946-226-4
ISBN 13: 978-0-87946-226-0

Printed in the United States of America

Year: 15 14 13 12 11 10 09 08 07
Printing: 15 14 13 12 11 10 9 8 7

Contents

Invitation to a Family Feast

Dear Parents,

You have overseen your child's first word, first step, first taste of solid food. You have shared your child's first day of school and the loss of the first tooth. Now you are on the brink of another first, a beautiful moment in your child's growth: First Holy Communion.

Not so long ago you saw to it that your child was initiated into the Catholic Church through baptism. You and other Christians celebrated the life of God in your child. But this was only the beginning of the church's formal initiation process. Receiving the Eucharist for the first time is the next step.

Each week the followers of Jesus gather as a family to celebrate the Eucharist (or the Mass), a sacrifice and a sacred meal in memory of him. There the saving acts of Jesus' passion, death and resurrection are made present again so that we can participate in them. There Jesus himself is really present and feeds us with his body and blood, nourishing the divine life in us. There we are united with him and with one another in his body, the church. There we develop the courage and determination to live like him in our corner of the world.

As a member of God's family, your child is invited to join us around the table of the Lord and to partake of this banquet by receiving Jesus in holy communion. You have the right and the responsibility to prepare your child for this sacrament. Your parish priests, teachers and other personnel will assist you and your child, but you are the major player in this sacred undertaking. Your words, attitudes and actions regarding the Eucharist influence your child in a powerful, irreplaceable way.

This book will help you carry out your momentous role. By reading it reflectively, you will deepen your understanding of Eucharist. You will update or refresh your knowledge of the guidelines and rituals for the communion. In addition, you will discover ways to make your child's First Holy Communion a treasured, memorable event.

Under your guidance, may your child know what a great and wondrous gift the Eucharist is and come to desire it with all his or her heart. May the faith you have passed on to your child grow and become strong. May your child's First Communion be the first of many communions until that day when we all feast at the heavenly banquet that has no end.

Special Meals in History

Think of a special meal you have recently enjoyed. Perhaps it was a quiet dinner for two, lunch with an old friend, a lively supper with the give–and–take of all family members. Maybe the occasion was a wedding, an anniversary, a funeral or Thanksgiving Day. Meals have meaning far beyond their biological function of nourishing our bodies!

Not only do we humans eat daily, but we eat with others to signify our togetherness, and we do it as a ritual to celebrate special events. Jesus knew what it means to be human. It is no wonder, then, that he chose a meal as the context for our worship. It *is* a wonder beyond words and a sublime mystery that at the Eucharist Jesus actually *becomes* our food and drink. He instituted this sacrament at the meal we call the Last Supper.

The Last Supper

The night before he died, Jesus gathered close friends for a farewell dinner. He gave them—and us—a distinctive way he would be with his followers always: the Eucharist. This was a precious gift, the gift of himself. During the meal Jesus took bread, said the traditional Jewish blessing over it, broke it and gave it to the disciples, saying, "Take and eat; this is my body which will be given for you. Do this in memory of me." Then he took a cup, gave thanks and gave it to them. He said, "This is my blood of the covenant, which will be shed for many for the forgiveness of sins."

With this ritual, the apostles became the first priests, and from the hands of Jesus himself they received the *first* First Communion. What great love Jesus showed for them and for us! At Mass, as the priest repeats Jesus' words and actions, bread and wine become the body and blood of Christ, through the power of the Holy Spirit.

Through the Eucharist, Jesus unites, nourishes, strengthens and guides his followers through the centuries. Moreover, just as Jesus sacrificed himself to the Father at the Last Supper and again the next day on the cross, so too at every Eucharist he again offers himself to his Father. This time we too are able to offer Jesus—and ourselves with him.

In the gospels of Matthew, Mark and Luke, it was the Passover meal that Jesus and his Jewish friends celebrated at the Last Supper.

The Passover Meal

For Jewish people, the Exodus event—their deliverance from slavery in Egypt—is God's supreme act of love for them. As slaves, the Israelites were forced to do hard labor and endure beatings and random killings. God freed them from this wretched life, made them a chosen people and gave them their own land.

The night Moses led the Israelites out of Egypt they ate a meal that God had prescribed. Each family slaughtered a lamb and marked their doorway with its blood. This blood was a sign that the tenth plague, death, should pass over their houses and not strike them. The Israelites ate the lamb with bitter herbs to commemorate the trials of their captivity and with bread that was unleavened because there was no time to wait for yeast to do its work. God commanded the Hebrews to observe forever a memorial feast of the liberating events. This feast is known as Passover and the meal as the Seder.

How appropriate that Jesus' sacred meal is associated with Passover. He is the Lamb of God whose blood has rescued us from the slavery of sin and death. Because he died and rose for us, we are able to "pass over" to the Father with him, to move from death to life in our promised land, heaven. The unleavened bread at our Eucharist is our bread of life. The wine is the blood that saves us. Jesus gave the Passover new, deeper meaning.

Manna

During the Israelites' forty-year journey to the promised land through the Sinai desert, God fed them with a special breadlike food called manna. It was a gift "rained down from heaven" that the hungry people found on the ground each morning, except for the Sabbath. Manna, a sign of God's presence, helped to keep the Israelites alive and gave them hope.

In our life's journey to our heavenly homeland, God sustains us in a similar way with the Eucharist, our bread from heaven. The manna was a foreshadowing, a hint, of the gift of the Eucharist.

The Multiplication of Loaves

Jesus further prepared his followers for the Eucharist by a miracle. All four gospels give an account of Jesus feeding thousands of people with only a few loaves of bread and some fish. As the meager food supply was distributed to the crowd, it multiplied miraculously. So abundant was the meal Jesus provided that not only was everyone filled but there were leftovers!

In John's gospel, after this amazing meal people followed Jesus, looking for more food. Jesus used the occasion to tell us the most intimate things about his gift of the Eucharist: He claimed to be the living bread from heaven and that whoever ate this bread would live forever. He said that the bread he would give was his flesh for the life of the world. He promised that whoever would eat his flesh or drink his blood would remain in him and he in them.

After this stunning revelation, many disciples left Jesus. They couldn't accept what he promised about feeding us with his own body and blood. But Jesus didn't take back his words or soften them. He didn't say, "Oh, come back. I was speaking only symbolically." We can assume that Jesus meant it when he said, "Whoever eats my flesh and drinks my blood has eternal life, and I will raise him on the last day" (John 6:54).

Emmaus

Another gospel story calls attention to the importance of the Eucharist. Three days after Jesus was crucified, two dejected disciples left Jerusalem for Emmaus. As they walked along, they tried to make sense out of the execution of the prophet Jesus. A stranger (the risen Jesus) joined them and explained what the scriptures said about the Messiah. When the three travelers reached Emmaus near evening, the disciples urged the stranger to stay with them. He accepted. At table he took bread, blessed it, broke it and gave it to them. In the breaking of the bread, they instantly recognized Jesus.

A Timeless Meal

Clearly, the memorial meal we celebrate claims a rich history and layers of meaning. In the Eucharist, past, present and future converge. Every time we celebrate the Eucharist, Jesus' past saving acts are made present and our future glory is promised. We have a foretaste of the eternal banquet when we will participate in the liturgy of heaven with the angels and saints. Our Eucharist is a sign of the "communion of saints" that we profess when we pray the Apostles Creed. We are even now united with those who have gone before us, one in faith.

Bread of Life and Cup of Salvation

The greatness of God is shown in God's willingness to become flesh. Divine love and mercy "compelled" God to become a human being, and in Bethlehem— a town whose name means "house of bread"—Jesus was born in a stable and laid in a manger, a feed box for animals. These details surrounding his birth fore- shadowed God's act of unimaginable generosity by which Jesus becomes our spiritual food and drink.

Unlike some of your friends and neighbors who may believe that the bread and wine at Mass are just sym- bols of Jesus, Catholics believe that Jesus is really and entirely present in each of the two elements. The bread and wine *become* the body and blood of Jesus. We believe that such is the immensity of God's un- fathomable love for us.

How is it possible that bread and wine are transformed into Jesus, whole and entire? Saint Augustine suggests that if God can create everything out of nothing, then God can just as surely change something already created into the body and blood of Jesus. This transformation occurs whenever a priest, acting in the person of Jesus, repeats what he did and said at the Last Supper. We call this change *transubstantiation*. This means that after the consecration—when the priest repeats Jesus' words "This is my body" over the bread and "This is my blood" over the wine—the *substance* of the bread and wine are changed, although they *appear* to be the same. They have become Jesus, whose body and blood, soul and divinity are actually present.

Just as food gives us nourishment to help us grow and be healthy, so the sacred food we receive in the Eucharist is essential for our spiritual life and health. Partaking of the body and blood of Christ nourishes God's life in us. We grow in faith, and our relationship with God and with others deepens. Through the Eucharist our venial (or lesser) sins are forgiven, and as we grow in union with Jesus we are morally strengthened to avoid serious sin in the future.

How completely appropriate it was that Jesus chose bread as one of the central elements of his memorial meal. In a humble way, just as at his birth, Jesus comes among us and nourishes us through this common food staple. And because bread is so abundant in every culture, the Eucharist can be celebrated all around the world. (Although bread can be baked with different flours such as wheat, barley, rye, oats, for the Eucharist we use only plain bread from wheat. It is also usually unleavened because at the Last Supper Jesus gave his disciples unleavened Passover bread.)

Likewise, wine is a beverage common to most cultures. It is a symbol of life and joy, traditionally used in celebrations. Recall the wedding feast at Cana when Jesus changed water into an abundance of choice wine. Moreover, wine is a symbol of salvation and of the new kingdom, which Jesus spoke of as a "wedding feast." The prophets Amos and Joel, speaking of the coming reign of God, said that the days are coming when the mountains will run with new wine.

In communion, God feeds us with the best of bread and the most excellent wine. For this sacred community meal, the altar is covered with a cloth and enhanced with candles and flowers. In some ways, it resembles our tables at home. The table of the Lord, though, also remains the altar of sacrifice.

The Perfect Sacrifice

Long ago, people worshiped God by offering the first fruits of the harvest and the first born of their animals. Through these sacrifices they praised and thanked God and pleaded for God's favor. We do the same at the sacrifice of the Mass. At Mass we thank—*Eucharist* means "thanksgiving"—and praise God for all creation and for all that God has done for us, especially the gift of his Son.

Bread and wine are the work of human hands, and they sustain us. We offer these gifts to the Father as symbols of our lives. The bread and wine are transformed into Jesus, who sacrifices himself to the Father for us. This is the perfect sacrifice, and it is the perfect way for us to praise and thank God. Then God returns our gifts to us in communion, and as we consume the transformed bread and wine we share in divine life.

Long ago the Israelites became God's chosen people by making a covenant, a solemn agreement with God. This covenant was sealed when Moses splashed the blood of a sacrificed animal on the altar and sprinkled the blood on the people. Our relationship with God was similarly established by a new, eternal covenant sealed by Christ's blood shed on the cross.

The elements of the Eucharist speak of sacrifice even by the way they come to be. The bread is made by crushing wheat grain; the wine is made by crushing grapes. On Calvary Jesus was "crushed" for our sins. His willingness to suffer and die brought about a new, glorified life that he shares with us. Saint Paul wrote, "For as often as you eat this bread and drink the cup, you proclaim the death of the Lord until he comes" (1 Corinthians 11:26).

Learn to savor how good
the LORD is.

Psalm 34:9

Union with Jesus Christ

Author Annie Dillard commented that if we truly realized the tremendous power unleashed at Mass we would all come wearing crash helmets. At the Eucharist we come in touch with the risen Lord and his saving acts that have renewed the cosmos. We might envy those people in first-century Israel who saw Jesus and heard him speak firsthand, but we are even more privileged because through the Eucharist we can meet Jesus in a very intimate manner, every day if we wish.

At Mass, Jesus is present in several ways. He is among us in the assembly of believers, which is his body. He assured us that wherever two or three are gathered in his name, he is in their midst. He is present as well in the priest and in the word of God proclaimed in the scriptures. But Jesus is most fully and especially present in the consecrated bread and wine. Perhaps you've said to a baby or a loved one, "I love you so much I could eat you up." In his love for us, Jesus actually allows us to consume him.

Communion means "in union with." Under the appearance of food and drink, Jesus is united with us and becomes part of us. We then become transformed to the degree that we allow Jesus to affect us. Gradually, we take on the characteristics of Jesus: his love and compassion, his sense of justice, his devotion to his Father. His life in us increases, and we become more like him—more Christ-like. In one of the Mass prayers, the priest prays, "May we come to share in the divinity of Christ who humbled himself to share in our humanity." The more we resemble Jesus, the more we are prepared to continue his work on

earth. Jesus used an image from nature to express this union with him. He told us, "I am the vine, you are the branches. Whoever remains in me and I in him will bear much fruit…" (John 15:5).

We are born with an innate hunger for God. Saint Augustine recognized this human longing and prayed, "Our hearts are restless until they rest in Thee." God has created and destined us to live forever in the divine presence. In communion we begin to experience this wonder. We are united with God in a special way, a foretaste of the union that will be everlasting in heaven. Communion satisfies our hunger, but in a way that can make us even hungrier for union with God.

Sacred hosts consecrated at Mass are reserved in our tabernacles in order that they may be carried as communion to the sick and dying. Christians with a serious illness and those who face surgery may be especially consoled and strengthened by this sacramental presence of Jesus. The dying are brought communion—called *viaticum*, "with you, on the way"—so that they may have Jesus with them in this intimate way during their final hours. In the reserved Blessed Sacrament, Jesus is with us in a special, physical way, even outside of Mass. We can pray to him there as though he were standing before us in all his glory.

Union with Others

Your child's First Communion is not a private affair or even only a family affair. It is an affair for the local faith community—the parish—and for the whole church.

The word "companion" is from the Latin *cum* (with) and *panis* (bread): A companion is someone with whom we break bread. Sharing a meal with someone is a sign of friendship, love and unity. Sitting around a table with family and friends, laughing and telling stories as we eat, celebrates and solidifies our relationships. To invite people to a meal at our home is to invite them to share our life. Our table, both at home and at the Eucharist, is a place of intimacy.

The Eucharist is the sign and source of Christian union. Whenever we gather at Mass to praise and thank God and to remember the saving acts of Jesus, we are bonded together more closely as the body of Christ. We come nearer his dream of perfect unity, the unity he prayed for at the Last Supper: "...that they may all be one, as you, Father, are in me and I in you, that they also may be in us, that the world may believe that you sent me" (John 17:21). The Eucharist makes us one family and energizes us with a sense of belonging to God and to one another.

Again, bread and wine are apt symbols for this unity. Just as many grains of wheat combine to form bread and many grapes to form wine, so too are many individuals brought together in faith to form the one body of Christ. It is like our singing during the communion procession—different voices combine to produce one song of praise, another

sign of our oneness in Jesus.

At our Eucharist we are united not only with the people who worship with us but also with the whole body of believers throughout the world. We are also united with the faithful who have gone before us, the lovers of God in heaven and those in purgatory.

Through communion all forms of human division should disappear. We must not let our prejudices or differences separate us, because, as Paul reminds us, "...you are all one in Christ Jesus" (Galatians 3:28). The more often we receive communion, the greater our love for one another will become. We will experience the deep peace and quiet joy that genuine, universal love brings.

If we are one, we are responsible for the other members of God's family.

God feeds us that we might feed one another. As Mother Teresa urged her sisters, "Let the people eat you up." In the story of the Last Supper in John's gospel, Jesus dramatizes in a striking way the attitude his followers must have. He washed and dried the feet of his disciples. He then said he was a model for us. We are to wash one another's feet, to serve others. The loving service we offer one another manifests our oneness in Jesus.

The Rite of Communion

As worshipers streamed into the aisles to form the communion procession, little Mickey asked, "Mom, when can I go up and get some?" Soon your child's days of staying quietly in the church pew will be over. He or she will be able to join the assembly in receiving Jesus in communion. This is possible because in 1910 Pope Pius X made a child-friendly change in church law. Considering Jesus' words, "Let the children come to me…" (Matthew 19:14), this pope concluded that young members of the church should be able to receive communion too, not just adults.

Another shift in thinking has lengthened communion lines. At one time so much stress was placed on the divinity of Christ in the Eucharist that people had a false sense of anxiety and unworthiness. They seldom received communion and did so only immediately after going to confession. Even saints did not receive communion more than a few times a year. Now, thank God, we regard receiving communion as an integral part of our participation in the Eucharist.

Let us now consider the steps of the Communion Rite of the Mass.

Our Father

After the Eucharist Prayer and its Great Amen, the Communion Rite opens with the perfect prayer Jesus gave us, the Our Father. As God's family, we stand around the table of the Lord and ask our Father for our daily bread. In some gatherings, the members hold hands during this prayer to show their relationship as brothers and sisters in Christ. So that we may be more worthy of receiving the heavenly bread, we beg forgiveness. Then the priest prays

that God might deliver us from evil, free us from sin and "...protect us from all anxiety as we wait in joyful hope for the coming of our Savior, Jesus Christ." Jesus came in history, he comes in the Eucharist, and we look forward to his coming at the end of time. We conclude this prayer: "For the kingdom, the power and the glory are yours, now and for ever."

Sign of Peace

As an immediate preparation for receiving communion, which is sometimes called "the sacrament of peace," the priest first prays to the Prince of Peace. Then he blesses us, "The peace of the Lord be with you always." We respond, "And also with you." We then turn to those around us and exchange a sign of peace, usually a handshake or a hug.

Breaking of the Bread

The priest breaks the host, as Jesus broke the bread at the Last Supper, and drops a small piece of it into the chalice. We address the Lamb of God, asking for mercy and peace. The priest then holds the host before us and declares, "This is the Lamb of God who takes away the sins of the world. Happy are those who are called to his supper." It is now communion time, when we are to be sacramentally united with Jesus.

We respond with a prayer of faith and love, announcing our unworthiness: "Lord, I am not worthy to receive you, but only say the word and I shall be healed." These words were first uttered by a Roman soldier who was pleading with Jesus to cure his servant. The soldier insisted that Jesus did not need to come to his home in order to heal. Like this humble man, we approach Jesus in faith, acknowledging that we are not fit to receive him into our heart, yet looking to him for healing from sin.

The Communion Procession

Those in the assembly who wish to receive communion approach the places where it is to be distributed, while a song is sung. Many parishes have returned to the practice of offering the people both the bread and the wine. In this way the symbolism of each element is better appreciated. After all, it was the blood of the Lamb that saved us.

In distributing communion the priest or Eucharistic Minister holds the host before us individually and announces, "The body of Christ" and also, if we are to drink from the cup,

"The blood of Christ." We answer, "Amen," which means "Yes, it is true." Our Amen at this moment is our act of faith in the reality of Jesus' presence. It also means that we say yes to Jesus and all he stands for; it is our commitment to him.

Conclusion and Commission

After communion there is silence or a song of praise. Then the celebrant prays that having been nourished at this sacred table we may live a life of faith and love. We respond, "Amen," which makes the prayer our own. The priest or deacon then bids us to go forth and *be* Eucharist, the presence of Christ, at home, in our neighborhood and in the world.

O sacred banquet in which Christ is received as food, the memory of his Passion is renewed, the soul is filled with grace and a pledge of the life to come is given to us.

Saint Thomas Aquinas

Growth in Jesus Christ

Saint Augustine exhorted the newly initiated, "Become what you eat, be what you are: the Body of Christ!" First Communion is a milestone in your child's journey of spiritual growth, but it marks only an early stage. Each succeeding celebration of the Eucharist will help your child become a vibrant member of the church. With your continued example and support, your child will develop into a person who carries the spirit of Christ into the world. The Eucharist will be not just a weekly routine but what Jesus meant it to be: a faith-filled experience that impacts daily life.

Here are seven ways you can foster your child's Christian growth:

1. *Pray.* Let your child see you praying. Pray together as a family. Continue or begin the customs of prayer before meals and night prayer. Before your child goes to bed, bestow a blessing by making the sign of the cross on his or her forehead. Set aside at least one day a week for family prayer and take turns leading it. Let prayer be part of your family custom to celebrate feasts and holidays and special family occasions.

2. *Celebrate Eucharist.* Go to church together for the Eucharist and sit up front! Read and talk about the scripture readings ahead of time. Afterwards discuss the homily. Your child will follow your lead, sensing whether you really value Mass or not.

3. *Read Scripture.* Invest in a family Bible if you don't have one. Read it together, a few verses each day, and let God speak directly to your hearts. Use it at family prayer gatherings.

4. *Make Sunday Special.* We observe Sunday as the Lord's Day because it is the day the Lord rose from the dead. Sunday is a day for celebrating life, especially by participating in the Eucharist. It is also a day for prayer, rest, fun and good works. It is a day for mending or strengthening relationships. Make it a point to do something as a family every Sunday.

5. *Reach Out.* Form your child into a Christian by doing spiritual and corporal works of mercy together as a family. For example, serve at a soup kitchen, donate extra clothes to the needy, visit the sick, tutor a student, or attend a wake service for a neighbor.

6. *Be Active in Your Parish.* Your Eucharistic celebration will be more meaningful for your family if you know the other participants and your lives are interwoven. Join parish committees, attend parish functions and volunteer for jobs. Model parish service for your child by serving as a reader, a Eucharistic Minister, a hospitality greeter or a choir member.

7. *Learn about Your Faith.* Go to workshops, lectures, missions and retreats. Purchase religious books, periodicals, videos and computer programs. The more you understand your faith, the stronger it will become and the more confidently and enthusiastically you will share it with your child.

Two maxims to keep in mind as you try to develop your child's faith: "Faith is caught more than taught" and "Actions speak louder than words." Nothing and no one will have more influence on your child than you, even though there are days when you may question this. These days prior to First Communion are a good time for you to do some solid thinking about your relationship with God and about your own faith and how you incorporate it into your home.

If Jesus is a valued member of your family, your child will come to know and love him as you do. If you show that the Christian life is precious to you, your child will imitate you. Just as your child favors you or your spouse in looks and personality, he or she will also reflect the characteristics of Christ that you bear in everyday life.

Forming another person into a saint is your awesome task as a parent and co-creator with God. Do you find this intimidating? Take heart. Our heavenly Father loves your child even more than you do and will be your silent partner in raising him or her. Through the Holy Spirit, you will all someday experience the truth of Jesus' words, "...I came so that they may have life and have it more abundantly" (John 10:10).

The ultimate miracle of Divine Love is this, that the life of the risen Christ is given us to give to one another through the daily bread of our human love.

Caryll Houselander

Questions and Answers

First Communion Day should be a day you, your family and your child enjoy. The following questions and answers should allay some concerns or fears and help make the day a pleasant experience.

Questions Parents May Have

When is my child ready to receive communion?

Any baptized person who realizes that the Eucharist is not ordinary bread and wine but the sacrament of Jesus' actual presence and who desires communion may receive it. This presupposes that the person knows that Jesus is our God and Savior. You, the parents, are in the best position to determine whether or not your child is ready.

My child is older than the children in the First Communion class. What can we do?

Talk to your parish priest or the Director of Religious Education. There may be provisions for older children through another program. Either a

special teacher or you yourself may be asked to prepare the child and be given the materials for it. Also, your child may be able to receive First Holy Communion privately, not as part of a communion group.

Must my child celebrate the sacrament of reconciliation before receiving communion?

In general, the sacrament of reconciliation is required before receiving the Eucharist only if a serious sin has been committed. It is a widely accepted tradition, however, that children celebrate the sacrament of reconciliation for the first time before their First Communion.

My spouse is not Catholic. How do I explain to my child why his or her mom or dad will not receive communion at the celebration of the Eucharist?

Tell your child that receiving communion in a Catholic liturgy is considered a sign of unity within the Catholic Church, and therefore for your spouse to receive communion would not be consistent with his or her own beliefs.

Because I am divorced, I have not been going to communion. Is it possible to receive communion when my child does?

What you think is something that keeps you from communion may not be such at all. Talk to a priest about your situation. He may clarify your position and, if you are remarried, suggest a way to make your current marriage valid in the eyes of the church.

I have not received communion for a long time, but I'd like to receive it with my child. What must I do?

If you have committed a serious sin, you must celebrate the sacrament of reconciliation first. After receiving absolution, you may receive communion. If you are not practicing your faith, you might find someone to talk to about your questions, past experiences, doubts and problems. Above all, pray for guidance.

My partner and I are not married, but we live together. What should we do on First Communion Day?

You might feel self-conscious about not receiving communion, especially if you are at a parish where parents and children sit together and then receive communion together. In this case, you might walk up with your child and then receive a blessing instead of communion. Ask a priest or catechist beforehand if this is possible. In any case, talk to your child ahead of time about why your situation keeps you from communion. Your child will be grateful for your honesty. Explain, for example, that right now you can't follow some of the rules that Catholics follow, so you can't go to communion. Just your presence on the exciting day will probably satisfy and please him or her. (Now, however, might be a good time for you to consider getting married.)

How often may Catholics receive communion?

We may receive communion whenever we celebrate the Eucharist, unless we are conscious of an unconfessed grave (or mortal) sin. We must receive communion at least once a year, preferably during the Easter season.

Questions Your Child Might Have

Here are some things your child might ask, along with some suggested answers.

How will Jesus fit in the host?

Jesus becomes present in the host in a mysterious way that we can't see with our eyes. Jesus can do anything, even change bread and wine into himself. Remember, he once fed more than five thousand people with only five loaves and two fish!

Am I really receiving Jesus?

Absolutely. You receive him just as he is today with his glorified, risen body.

How long does the bread and wine remain the body and blood of Jesus after it is consecrated?

The bread and wine remain the body and blood of Jesus until they are consumed and digested.

If I receive just the sacred bread and not the sacred wine, will I receive only part of Jesus?

No. Jesus is wholly present in the bread and wholly present in the wine. When you receive the host, you receive Jesus completely. In the same way, Jesus is completely in every part of the bread and wine. Therefore, if you receive only part of a host, you still receive Jesus entirely.

Is it all right to chew the host?

Yes, just the way you chew ordinary food.

How can we all be receiving Jesus at the same time?

Jesus is God and can do anything. Moreover, his body is very different from ours. When he was on earth he had a body like ours. Now that he is in heaven, Jesus has what we call a "glorified body" and can be in many places at the same time.

Do I have to celebrate reconciliation each time before I receive holy communion?

No. You can receive communion as long as you haven't committed a very serious sin. Someone your age is not likely to commit such sins.

What should I say to Jesus after receiving communion?

Talk to Jesus as your friend and savior. Thank him for coming to you. Praise and thank him for all he has done for you. Tell him how much you love him. Ask him to forgive you if you have not been a loving child as he wishes. Ask him to help you to be like him. Tell Jesus anything you wish to tell him, such as your special desires or things you're worried about. Speak from your heart.

Does it make any difference if I receive Jesus from a priest or from a Eucharistic Minister?

No. Jesus is still present in the sacred bread and wine, no matter who distributes communion.

What if I drop the host or spill the wine?

There is little chance that this will happen, but if it does, the person who gave you the host or the cup will help you.

Will I be any different after receiving communion?

You will look and feel the same, and you probably won't act very different at first. Gradually though, after receiving Jesus many times, you ought to become more like him and be a better Christian.

Just as the bread, which is made from the earth, when God is invoked is no longer common bread but the Eucharist, both earthly and heavenly, so our bodies, after we have received the Eucharist, are no longer corruptible, since they hold the hope of the resurrection.

Saint Irenaeus

How Can I Help Prepare My Child?

In the *National Catechetical Directory for Catholics of the United States* we find this statement: "Parents have a right and duty to be intimately involved in preparing their children for First Communion" (#122). You taught your child what it means to belong to the human family: to talk, walk and eat, to be polite and honest, to respect people and their belongings. Now you are called to introduce your child to an important stage of life in God's family: worshipping God at the celebration of the Eucharist.

The catechists at your parish have been explaining to your child the meaning of the Eucharist, the parts of the Mass, how to receive communion. This does not necessarily mean that your child has learned this information completely! To reinforce what was taught, it is good to review with your child each week the lessons in the religion book. Ask questions and invite him or her to ask you questions. To insure that your child's First Communion Day is a day of peace and joy, you can allay some fears and concerns by practicing in the following ways:

Receiving the Bread: Obtain a few unconsecrated hosts from your parish so your child can see what the bread will taste and feel like. Make sure your child knows that Jesus is not really present in the practice host. An alternative is to use a bit of food similar to the host in size and shape. You can use this "host" to practice the method of receiving that your child has chosen to use. There are two options:

Method 1: On the tongue. In this case see that your child extends his or her tongue far enough. Explain that after the host is placed on the tongue, it may be chewed and swallowed as any other food.

Method 2: In the hand. We set our left hand on our right hand. We form a "throne" out of our hands, Saint Augustine said. Then we step to the side and use our right hand to place the host in our mouth. (Left-handed people set their right hand on their left hand and then use their left hand to place the host in the mouth.)

Instruct your child to look at the sacred host when it is held up. After the minister says, "The Body of Christ," the child responds "Amen" and then receives the sacred host.

Receiving the Wine: Even if your child may not be receiving from the cup on the day of First Communion, make sure he or she knows how to do it. After the minister says, "The Blood of Christ," your child responds "Amen" and then takes the cup. Instruct him or her to take the cup with both hands and take a sip of the sacred wine.

If your child has never drunk wine, provide a sample. Some children find wine bitter and distasteful. Knowing what it's like ahead of time will prevent surprise and avoid an undesirable reaction.

Practice receiving the host and the cup until your child feels comfortable doing it.

Some Reminders for Your Child

- We walk to and from communion with hands joined and with reverence, not looking around or interacting with other people.

- We fast from food for an hour before communion, although water and medicine are allowed. (Often an hour elapses between the time we leave home for Mass and the time we receive communion, but children should still know this rule.)

- We do not eat candy or chew gum before receiving communion.

- We receive communion with clean hands out of respect for Jesus.

Go to Mass with your child regularly before First Communion Day and help him or her follow what is happening. Sit where your child can easily see. Afterwards talk about what took place. Practice some of the prayers and responses with your child so that he or she can participate more fully and confidently in the Eucharist.

Help your child make a good First Communion by entering into the preparation in special ways. Here are some ideas:

1. Talk to your child about your own First Communion. What does communion mean to you today?

2. Explain how important communion has been to other people. For example, Saint Julie Billiart said about her own First Communion Day, "Never in my life have I experienced such wonder and joy as I felt that day." (Your child's reaction to the First Communion experience may not be as heightened as the saint's was, however. Aside from enjoying being the center of a celebration, your child may not be particularly elated about the spiritual aspect of the occasion. So don't exaggerate expectations, leading him or her to think something was wrong if it wasn't the greatest event of life.)

3. Encourage your child to prepare his or her heart to receive Jesus. For a period of time before the big day, plan together a daily good deed that your child can do as a way to prepare. Here are some ideas for one week:

Monday: Call or visit Grandma.
Tuesday: Pray an extra Hail Mary.
Wednesday: Be cheerful all day.

Thursday: Do something kind for someone.
Friday: Spend a minute thinking of Jesus' love for you.
Saturday: Help with housecleaning.
Sunday: Express thanks to someone.

4. Help your child anticipate First Communion Day. On a calendar draw a host and a simple chalice in each square about a week before First Communion Day. At the end of each day, let your child color the chalice yellow. This might be part of a night prayer ritual that includes a prayer such as: "Jesus, I can hardly wait to receive you. Bless me and make me more deserving of this honor each day."

5. Have your child write a prayer expressing a desire to receive Jesus.

6. On the days before First Communion Day, hold a family novena or triduum of prayer for your first communicant. See Prayers for Communion (pp. 71–76) for sample prayer services.

7. Make a visit to the Blessed Sacrament with your child. Suggest that your child tell Jesus how much he or she is looking forward to the day of First Communion. Point out the sanctuary light that tells us that Jesus is present.

8. Bake bread with your child and enjoy eating it with the whole family. Use prepared dough or a recipe such as this one:

1/2 cup (one stick) butter or oil
1 cup water
1/2 cup honey
2 cups white flour
1 1/2 cups wheat flour
1/2 tsp. salt
1/2 tsp. baking soda
1/2 tsp. baking powder

Combine the first three ingredients in a bowl. Combine all the dry ingredients in a larger bowl; mix thoroughly. Add liquid ingredients to the dry, and then blend. Knead lightly. Roll out on a floured board and cut or shape to desired size. The dough should be flat, not shaped like a loaf. It may be scored for easy breaking. Bake on an ungreased cookie sheet at 375 degrees for 10 to 15 minutes. Time will depend on the thickness of the dough; edges will be brown when the bread is done.

No doubt before First Communion Day your parish will have at least one meeting for parents. If at all possible, be there. If not, see that someone from the family is present or find out what happened at the meeting. Participate wholeheartedly in any preparatory activities the parish plans for your child and family. Your presence at these activities will highlight the importance of the occasion in your child's eyes.

As you prepare your child for First Communion, keep in mind that you are also preparing him or her for the whole Christian life.

How Can We Celebrate the Event?

Brenda will never forget her daughter's First Communion. At the offertory collection her husband took out bills amounting to some two hundred dollars. The money was for pizza, cake and other goodies for the party afterwards. Intending to give the money to Brenda so she could put a few dollars in the collection, the husband handed the entire roll of bills to their daughter, sitting between them. The girl promptly deposited the entire amount in the basket. The parents were too surprised and embarrassed to ask for the money back! There are cheaper ways, however, to make your child's First Communion a memorable experience. The following are a few ideas that you may wish to include in your family's celebration.

Before the Day

Let your child help write and send invitations to the First Communion Mass and to a First Communion party. You might plan two parties: one for the family and one for other relatives and friends. You might also consider a party for your child and several friends who have also made their First Communion.

Include your child's godparents as you plan this special occasion. They might like to have a private meal with your child. If they live at a distance, arrange to have them call your child during or before the party in honor of his or her First Communion.

Invite the parish priest and your child's teacher to the First Communion party. Even if they cannot attend, they will be honored and pleased to be asked.

New clothes are symbols of new life. Provide a special outfit or some special item of clothing for your child for First Communion. Depending on your parish customs, girls may wear white dresses and veils; boys may wear white shirts and ties. Find out what is required. The clothes do not have to be expensive to be special. And they should not overshadow the reception of communion itself.

On the evening before the day of First Communion, celebrate with a festive family meal. Enhance the meal with a special tablecloth, linen napkins, placemats, name cards, candles and a centerpiece that includes bread and wine. Serve your child's favorite dishes. Play soft background music. To emphasize the importance of the event, dress up yourselves. One child's parents appeared in a tuxedo and evening gown for the occasion!

Work together to make a family banner with the Eucharistic symbols of bread and wine. This can be displayed during the party.

Unearth mementos of your child's baptism: photos, the white garment and candle. Go through the photos and reminisce about the baptism day. Display the baptism items at the First Communion party.

Write a letter to your child that you will present on the day of First Communion. In the letter mention ways that he or she has become more like Jesus. Express your wish that your child grow stronger in faith and closer to Christ each day. Assure your child of your love, support and prayers.

On the Day

You and the rest of your family might offer up the Mass that day in thanksgiving for your first communicant and for his or her being part of your family. Announce at breakfast that this is the family's intention for the Eucharist.

Take photos or make a video of the day. Find out if your parish has a policy regarding cameras in church. Some parishes have class photos taken.

If you are not in the habit of receiving communion, make an effort to do so on that day. This will add to your child's delight.

Because of our culture, children may brag about how much money they received for First Communion. Keep your gift in tune with the religious nature of the celebration. Give your child a Bible, a prayer book, a rosary, a crucifix, a medal, a framed religious picture, a statue or other religious item. You might suggest that your child donate to the hungry, to the church or to another worthy cause part of any gift money received.

You might purchase a special First Communion cake or bake one yourself. (For one in the shape of a host, use a small round pan. For a chalice shape, use a square pan and cut the cake on the diagonal. Join the two points of the triangles together.)

At the party, guide your child to light the baptism candle. Pray a grace before the meal. Invite the guests to pray for blessings on your child.

After the Day

Let your child wear First Communion clothes for the next Sunday Mass or two.

Arrange to have a professional photo taken of your child wearing the clothes worn on First Communion Day. Give prints to godparents, grandparents and other relatives and friends.

Assemble the photos of the day in a special album.

Talk to your child about the day, giving him or her an opportunity to savor the moments and to express joy and gratitude.

Fundamentally the Eucharist is a victory, a victory of one who is absent to become present in a world that conceals him.

Saint Cyril of Alexandria

Scripture Readings for Communion

You have prepared for your child's First Communion by reading this book. Another way you can prepare is to read and reflect on the following related scripture passages and reflections. Arrange some private time to read a passage and the comments that follow it. Then consider what the passage means to you and your life. Let your thoughts give rise to resolutions that will help you be a better Christian parent for your child. You may record your resolutions on page 79. Every now and then, read your resolutions and review how you are keeping them.

We Are the Body of Christ

> The cup of blessing that we bless, is it not a participation in the blood of Christ? The bread that we break, is it not a participation in the body of Christ? Because the loaf of bread is one, we, though many, are one body, for we all partake of the one loaf.
> 1 Corinthians 10:16–17

We have an expression, to "walk in the other person's shoes." The gift of the Eucharist so identifies us with Jesus that it is as though he were walking in our shoes, or we in his sandals. Jesus himself said this in other words: "Whoever eats my flesh and drinks my blood remains in me and I in him" (John 6:56).

Through us, Jesus becomes present to the people we meet every day. Through us, he still preaches the good news, calms storms, feeds the hungry, prays, heals, and yes, still suffers. Through us, Jesus continues to bring about God's kingdom of justice and peace.

If we are one with Jesus through the Eucharist, we are also one with everyone else who shares in this sacred meal. This has serious implications. It means that we must see the face of Jesus in the face of others and treat them with love.

A story illustrates the love that believing Christians manifest for one another. A man had a vision of hell. People were seated at tables laden with food. However, everyone was starving because the only way they could eat was to use three-foot-long chopsticks. Then the man had a vision of heaven. There too people were at a feast with the same daunting chopsticks. They, however, were having a grand time enjoying the banquet. They were feeding one another with the chopsticks!

God Feeds the People

> God rained manna upon them
> for food;
> bread from heaven he
> gave them.
> All ate a meal fit for heroes;
> food he sent in abun-
> dance.
> Psalm 78:24–25

God sustained the Israelites on their desert trek by a "bread" that appeared miraculously. Like them, we are on a perilous journey to our promised land. God also provides heavenly bread for us, far beyond anything we could have imagined. We can't understand this miracle

any more than the Israelites understood God's care for them. All we can do is be grateful—and perhaps not surprised—that God loves us so extravagantly.

Jesus Multiplies Food

When Jesus raised his eyes and saw that a large crowd was coming to him, he said to Philip, "Where can we buy enough food for them to eat?" He said this to test him, because he himself knew what he was going to do. Philip answered him, "Two hundred days' wages worth of food would not be enough for each of them to have a little [bit]." One of his disciples, Andrew, the brother of Simon Peter, said to him, "There is a boy here who has five barley loaves and two fish; but what good are these for so many?" Jesus said, "Have the people recline." Now there was a great deal of grass in that place. So the men reclined, about five thousand in number. Then Jesus took the loaves, gave thanks, and distributed them to those who were reclining, and also as much of the fish as they wanted. When they had had their fill, he said to his disciples, "Gather the fragments left over, so that nothing will be wasted." So they collected them, and filled twelve wicker baskets with fragments from the five barley loaves that had been more than they could eat.

John 6:5–13

Jesus hosted a picnic for a crowd in which *men alone* totaled five thousand. He did it using a boy's bread and fish that Andrew had discovered. Jesus feeds us in the Eucharist so that we can feed others. We are to be a Eucharistic people and live Eucharistic lives. People are hurting, and Jesus says, "Feed them." People long for justice, and Jesus says, "Feed them." People are lonely, and Jesus says, "Feed them."

We might ask, "What good are my gifts in the face of such enormous world needs?" And Jesus says, "Remember the boy's donation. You do what you can, your two percent, and I'll take care of the rest. I'll multiply your efforts." Trust Jesus. He has a good track record.

Jesus Offers Eternal Life

"I am the bread of life. Your ancestors ate the manna in the desert, but they died; this is the bread that comes down from heaven so that one may eat it and not die. I am the living bread that came down from heaven; whoever eats this bread will live forever; and the bread that I will give is my flesh for the life of the world."

The Jews quarreled among themselves, saying, "How can this man give us [his] flesh to eat?" Jesus said to them, "Amen, amen, I say to you, unless you eat the flesh of the Son of Man and drink his blood, you do not have life within you. Whoever eats my flesh and drinks my blood has eternal life, and I will raise him on the last day. For my flesh is true food and my blood is true drink. Whoever eats my flesh and drinks my blood re-

mains in me and I in him."
John 6:48–56

Life is so sweet and rich at times that we dread its ending. We yearn to live forever. We hope there is more to life beyond our death. The thought of no longer existing is abhorrent. Jesus experienced that hunger for life, and he told us that our deepest yearning will be fulfilled! We can live forever. What's more, Jesus gave us a means of attaining it. We don't have to search for a precious stone, travel to a foreign land, climb a treacherous mountain or pay an enormous sum for eternal life. Jesus invites us to participate in the Eucharist and live Eucharistic lives, and that alone will give us eternal life.

How consoling it is to know that our family members and friends who have eaten at the Lord's table on earth can now be partaking of the heavenly banquet—and even more consoling, when we face the inevitability of our own death, to know that Jesus will raise us up on the last day. He promised that, and God is ever faithful.

The heart preparing for Communion should be as a crystal vial filled with clear water in which the least mote of uncleanness will be seen.

Saint Elizabeth Ann Seton

Prayers for Communion

Prayer of Desire for First Communion

Dear Jesus, I can hardly wait until you come to me in communion. How good and loving you are to invite me to receive you! Thank you for this gift of yourself. I love you. Help me prepare my heart for your visit by loving you and others more each day. Amen.

Family Bread and Grape Juice Ritual before First Communion Day

[Set the family table with candles and a special tablecloth or table mats. As the centerpiece, have bread in a basket and grape juice in a transparent pitcher.]

Leader: We are looking forward to *(name's)* First Communion Day. During this prayer ritual we will think about the beauty and joy of this day and pray for *(name)*. Please respond to each prayer: "Thank you, Jesus."

Jesus, on the night before you died for us, you gave us the gift of the Eucharist...

At Mass, our bread and wine become your sacred body and blood...

In communion you come within us...

In communion we are united with you and with all the members of your church...

Through communion we grow in your life and are made holy by your grace...

Through communion our sins are forgiven and we are strengthened to be good Christians...

Leader: Let us now extend our hands in blessing toward *(name)* as we pray. After each prayer respond, "Bless *(him, her)*, Jesus."

That *(name)* may understand how wonderful communion is...

That *(name)* may receive you with a heart full of thanks and love...

That *(name)* may grow to become more like you each day...

That *(name)* may know the joy of being part of your body, the church…

Amen.

[Pass the bread and pour the grape juice and enjoy one another's company.]

Family Novena before First Communion Day

Have a countdown to First Communion Day by praying a novena (a nine-day prayer) as a family for your first communicant. For each of the nine days before the First Communion, pray the respective prayer below.

Blessing: At the end of each daily prayer, the parents and any siblings bless the first communicant on the forehead with the sign of the cross, with holy water if possible.

You might do this before dinner together each evening.

Ninth Day Before

Parent(s): Jesus, you love *(name)* very much. You saved *(him, her)* from sin and death by dying on the cross and rising. Through baptism *(he, she)* became God's child. In nine days you will come to *(name)* in communion. Fill *(him, her)* with thanksgiving for this great gift. Let our prayers help prepare *(him, her)* to receive you.

Child: Jesus, help me prepare my heart for you.

Eighth Day Before

Parent(s): Jesus, you died for our sins. We remember this in the Eucharist. In eight days *(name)* will receive the sacred bread and wine of communion. This is your body and blood that you gave for us. Keep *(name)* free from sin and full of grace.

Child: Jesus, help me prepare my heart for you.

Seventh Day Before

Parent(s): Jesus, by your death and rising you won everlasting life for us. In seven days *(name)* will receive you, the risen Lord, in communion. Let *(name)* always live so that someday *(he, she)* may be happy with you forever in heaven.

Child: Jesus, help me prepare my heart for you.

Sixth Day Before

Parent(s): Jesus, in the Eucharist you nourish the divine life we received in baptism. In six days *(name)* will receive you for the first time in holy communion. Help *(him, her)* grow in love of you so that *(he, she)* lives as a true child of God.

Child: Jesus, help me prepare my heart for you.

Fifth Day Before

Parent(s): Jesus, in communion you come closer to us than anyone can ever be. As our food and drink you become one with us. In five days *(name)* will welcome you in *(his, her)* heart. May *(he, she)* come to love you more and more each day.

Child: Jesus, help me prepare my heart for you.

Fourth Day Before

Parent(s): Jesus, you want all your followers to be united in love. Through the Eucharist you bind us all together in friendship and love. In four days *(name)* will be more closely joined to the church through holy communion. Give *(him, her)* the grace to be an active member of the church.

Child: Jesus, help me prepare my heart for you.

Third Day Before

Parent(s): Jesus, *(name)* was initiated into your church at baptism. *(He, she)* is looking forward to further initiation through the Eucharist. In three days *(name)* will receive

this sacrament of initiation. Make *(him, her)* a good Catholic Christian, full of faith and love.

Child: Jesus, help me prepare my heart for you.

Second Day Before

Parent(s): Jesus, in the Eucharist you make us more like you. In two days you will come to *(name)* in communion. Enable *(him, her)* to be the person of kindness, compassion, wisdom and courage that you were. Increase *(his, her)* faith, hope and love.

Child: Jesus, help me prepare my heart for you.

The Day Before

Parent(s): Jesus, tomorrow will be a day of great joy. *(Name)* will receive you in holy communion for the first time. *(He, she)* will know how much you love us. Bless *(name)* and make *(him, her)* a strong, loving Christian. May *(name)* always long to receive you in the Blessed Sacrament. May *(he, she)* always appreciate all you have done for us.

Child: Jesus, help me prepare my heart for you.

Family Triduum before First Communion Day

[If the family novena is not feasible for some reason, you may wish to conduct a triduum (a three-day prayer). On the three days before First Communion Day, pray the last three services of the preceding novena, one each day.]

Prayer after Communion

Jesus, I love you with my whole heart. Thank you for all your gifts, especially for the gift of yourself in communion. I'm sorry for the times I have not been loving. Help me to live the way you want me to. Fill me with your life so that I can carry your love into the world.

Prayer of Spiritual Communion

Jesus, I desire your presence in my soul very much. Since I cannot now receive you in the Eucharist, come into my heart spiritually. I know you are always with me. I embrace you and unite myself with you. Never permit me to be separated from you.

The Eucharist is the Church
at her best.

Gabriel Moran

Resolutions for Parents

To better help my child prepare for First Communion and to better celebrate the Eucharist with my child now and in the future, I resolve the following:

1. _____

2. _____

3. _____

4. _____

5. _____

Other Books in This Series

THE GIFT OF BAPTISM
TOM SHERIDAN

A welcoming book that teaches parents about the meaning of the sacrament and helps them understand their role as parents. 64 pages, paperback, $4.95

THE GIFT OF CONFIRMATION
SISTER KATHLEEN GLAVICH

Explanation and suggestions for parents of children being confirmed, including much of the information contained in *The Gift of Confirmation Sponsors*. 80 pages, paperback, $4.95

THE GIFT OF THE ANOINTING OF THE SICK
SISTER KATHLEEN GLAVICH

A preparation guide for those preparing for this sacrament, as well as their family members and close friends. 64 pages, paperback, $4.95

THE GIFT OF GODPARENTS
TOM SHERIDAN

Information about the sacrament of baptism and the responsibilities of godparenting are blended with touching stories and suggestions. 96 pages, paperback, $5.95

THE GIFT OF CONFIRMATION SPONSORS
SISTER KATHLEEN GLAVICH

Explanation and suggestions for those chosen to be sponsors for children being confirmed, including much of the information contained in *The Gift of Confirmation,* but aimed specifically at sponsors. 80 pages, paperback, $4.95

THE GIFT OF RECONCILIATION
SISTER KATHLEEN GLAVICH

Presents to parents the meaning and importance of confession, penance and reconciliation for their children—and themselves. 80 pages, paperback, $4.95

Available from booksellers or call 800-397-2282